ONG-

etles
eat!

D1331824

01381

Also available:
Airmail from Africa
Ngorongoro – Where Cow Poo is Lucky!
Michael Cox

Coming soon:
Airmail from South America
Amazonia – Where Tree Frogs go Moo!
Michael Cox

AIRMAIL FROM...

BAN PONG -
where beetles taste great!

Michael Cox

Illustrated by
Rhian Nest James

Hippo

Scholastic Children's Books,
Commonwealth House, 1-19 New Oxford Street,
London WC1A 1NU, UK

A division of Scholastic Ltd
London ~ New York ~ Toronto ~ Sydney ~ Auckland
Mexico City ~ New Delhi ~ Hong Kong

Published in the UK by Scholastic Ltd, 1999

ISBN 0 439 01221 X

Typeset by M Rules
Printed by Cox & Wyman, Reading, Berks

2 4 6 8 10 9 7 5 3 1

Ban Pong - where beetles taste great! is part of a series of books about fascinating countries around the world. Each book is made up of letters written by a boy or girl who lives in one of these countries. You might find that their English isn't always quite right (unlike yours, which is always perfect - ha ha!). So watch out for a few mistakes and crossings out. Sometimes in their letters the children use words from their own language (just like we all do!).

When you see a Thai language word in this book, don't run and hide behind your settee! Just sound the word out like you did when you were first learning to read English, like this... K-R-U-N-G T-H-E-P. See, didn't hurt a bit, did it? Your friends will be dead impressed (unless they happen to come from Thailand, of course!).

21 August

Hello dear reader!

My name is Srinthip Prajom and I live in Ban Pong which is in Thailand, South East Asia. Here it is on a map so you will know where I am.

The other day a boy in my class told me that he writes letters to friends in places all over the world. He said that these children are called his pen-friends and that they write letters back to him and send him things also. "That sounds like really good fun!" I thought to myself. "I would also like to do that and have lots of friend-pens too!"

So that is why I am writing this letter to you: I

have decided that I am going to be your friend-pen. I hope you don't mind!

After today I will be sending you all sorts of letters and stuff from Thailand and telling you lots of stories about things that happen to me, some funny and some sad. I hope you enjoy them! I think that this will be good sanuk for both of us. For you because you will find out interesting things about me and my country and maybe one day you will be coming for your holiday. And for me because I will be getting practised to write and speak my English properly. By the way, "sanuk" is our word for fun, which we are all absolutely crazy about here!

Uh oh! I was just going to tell you all about me and my family but it looks like I have to stop writing now. Mum is calling me to collect the eggs from our ducks! I stare forward to speaking to you soon.

Your very good pal,

Srinthip Prajom

PS All my friends call me Shrimp, so you can too.

2 September

Dear friend from over-the-seas,

Sawadeee! Hello once more again. It's me, your pal Shrimp. Pen yangai? That means "How are you?" I hope you are feeling well and that you got my last letter all right. I posted it special airmail. Now that you are my proper pen-friend I suppose you will probably want to nosey a bit more about me – so I will tell you!

I am nine years old and a girl. I was born on 5 December in Krung Thep which is the capital city of Thailand – I think you call it Bangkok.

I'm one metre and 42 centimetres tall and I weigh 40 kilos. I've got black hair, brown eyes and lightly brown skin. Sometimes I like to wear nice fashion clothes but a lot of the time I have on cotton

This is me ↘

trousers and T-shirts or my school uniform. My favourite hobbies are dancing, drawing and writing. I go to Ban Pong Primary School and I enjoy all of my lessons (well, nearly all!). When I grow up I would like to be a doctor or a beauty queen (but both together would be best!).

Introducing Miss Shrimp, doctor and beauty queen

I live in a big wooden house on legs with my mum, whose name is Chookiet, and my dad, who is called Tek. My mum is a business lady who does tourist work and my dad is a doctor. Mum and Dad can speak English quite good so they will be very helpful for my writings to you.

I have also got two brothers. One is called Decha, he is nearly five and his nickname is Lek, and the other is Aroon, he is eleven and his nickname is Frog. Frog is a really good artist and wants to be a cartoon drawer when he grows up. He says that he will do some pictures for you (he is a good big brother to me!). My grandma also lives with us. She is called Santipap and is 62 years old, and is very wise! Frog has drawn this family picture for you so that you can see what we all look like:

Our House *Dad* *Mum* *Grandma* *Frog* *Lek* *Shrimp* *Yip* *Pip* *Our ducks*

We've got a dog called Yip and a cat called Pip, also twelveteen ducks, but they haven't all got names! Pip is a Siamese cat. Siam is the old name for Thailand and these special sort of cats were made here first. She has a pretty face and big dark coloured ears and is very, very small. There are not hardly many Siamese cats now in Thailand but in other parts of the world there are quite a lot. Do you have them? Yip is just a mix-up all-sorts dog, very big, but nice and friendly – unless you are a ~~burger~~ burglar coming to rob us!

On the next page is Frog's picture of our animals.

Pip ↓ Yip ↘ One of our ducks ↙

My best friend at school is Duang Dao Utarnwuthipong, but you can call her Finch. Her mum is a basket maker and her dad is a noodle.* I was going to tell you some more things but I must stop writing now. My hand is aching and I can hear my little brother Lek calling from our garden. He's making a very big noise. I wonder what can the matter be? I'll write again soon!

Best wish,

Shrimp

P.S Frog has drawn this picture of our house and village from a bird eye view — well, from up the big rain tree in our garden actually! I did the labels — sorry about the scribbles (that was Lek trying to help!).

* My friend Finch's dad is not a noodle. I should have writed he is a noodle seller. Sorry, sorry Mr Utarnwuthipong!

6 September

Dear pen-friend,

Hi, it's me again! Letter number three already! It is a big one. I have got lots to say to you! First of all, since I last wrote I have been thinking that I should tell you some things for you to enjoy when you come to Thailand! So here are my lists of exciting treasures with some great drawings by my brother, Mr Artist Frog!

NATURE THINGS THAT WE HAVE GOT

❍ Big mountains and rain forests with monkeys, elephants, tigers, snakes (some as long as hose pipes!), giant insects, spiders (size of dinner plates!), birds, flowers, all kinds!

2) Warm seas all swimming with octopus, turtles, sharks, squids, flying fishes and much, much more. Jump in, most of them will not hurt you!

3) Tropical weather. Definitely no need to bring your big overcoats.* We are hot all the year, but with quite a lot of very big rain in some months.

(*We do get a little bit of cool – but this is only in the North when the dry season is on – so don't worry about it.)

4) Thousands of fields full of water and hard-working farm people with big hats and water buffaloes (sometimes with big fish also!). These are rice paddies where we grow our delicious Thailand rice. Do you eat it in your home?

Quack quack! Oink!

flutter flutter cluck!

Squeak! Croak!

5) Even more interesting animals everywhere you go. Ducks, geese, pigs, hens, flying lizards, bats, ants, flying foxes, glow worms, butterflies and frogs and toads – all over the places – in your garden, under your house, behind your cupboard, on your ceiling and in your sink.

PEOPLE THINGS THAT WE HAVE GOT

1) Wooden houses standing on stilts, many standing with other ones in a nice, friendly little crowd (called a compound). Also houses floating on water and shops floating on water. Many houses with beautiful, curvy bits on them.

2) Children, mum, dad, gran, grandad, aunties, uncles, cousins, all living together in the compound houses to make one big happy family (like mine!). And people having sanuk fun all over the place! Parades, celebrations, games, parties and festivals nearly all the time in Thailand. We are fun mad!

3) Beautiful Buddha statues and also monks nearly everywhere you go. Buddha is very important for almost all Thai people.

4) Lovely big temples called wats in nearly every village, more than 30,000 altogether. The monks live in them and we visit.

5) Mouth watering things for everyone to eat. All sorts very fresh from our forests and gardens: banananas (17 kinds!), sweet rice, roast pigs, coconut ice cream, juicy pineapples, melons pieces with crushed ice, barbecue lobsters, ~~spacey spikey~~ spicy sauces and lots, lots more.

bananas
sweet rice
coconut ice cream
roast pig
pineapple
melon with crushed ice
lobster

These are just a few of the fine things that we have got. I hope it does not make you too jealous of me. There are thousands more as well, I will tell you about them in my new letters!

Now, what else was I going to tell you? Oh yes, remember that big kerfluff and noise we had in our garden the last time I wrote to you? Well, that was my brother, Lek. He had been playing with his ball but it went into the wild part behind the bamboo fence so he went to find it. When he pushed the big grasses apart he came face on face with a giant snake! It was two metres along and nearly as

Where's that naughty ball gone?

thick as a car tyre! Poor Lek was petrified, but not hurt, thank goodness!

When mum went to look the snake had gone. We think it might be a ~~pithon~~ python (we get them here you know). They wrap around little animals to crush them for eating. Sometimes even little childrens too, so Grandma says! I got the shudders just thinking about it. From now on we're all going to have to keep our eyes skinnied!

Best wishings,

Shrimp

19 September

Dear pen-friend from the cold place,

Sanuk mai? How are your doings? Have you been to school today? I have, but in a few weeks it will be time for our school holidays. When are yours? In class this morning we had to do a really hard spelling test, not in writing like this but in Thai which looks like this:

ศิรินทิพย์ ประจอม

That's my name in Thai! Can you write it? I wonder what your name would look like in Thai? I think it might be quite hard for you to write!

Did you know we have got 76 letter shapes in our alphabet! Yes, 50 more than yours. More for us to learn at school! As well as having different writing from you we also have different talking. When you hear it we might sound like we are saying nonsense. It was the same when I first heard English, it came in my ears like a jumble of goobledegok. But not any more!

Actually I think our talking is also a bit quieter than yours. To help you a bit I am putting some useful words with this letter. You can do a practice if you like, but don't worry if you get them wrong!

Now to another thing. I am a real scatterbrain at times, my head is so fill with things to tell you that some of them are nearly getting lost. When I told you about my family I forgot to tell you about a very special person who is sometimes here with us in Ban Pong. He is my Uncle Boon. Well, he's my Dad's uncle actually.

Most of the time Uncle Boon is in Bangkok where he drives a tuk-tuk. Do you have these? They are little taxi cars with only three wheels, you will see them all over the place in Bangkok when you come here. They are called tuk-tuk because of the terrible noise that comes from them. Uncle Boon is really proud of his. It is very beautiful in all colours: red, purple, green, orange and yellow stripey, plus lots of silver decorations. He calls it Jet and is always rubbing it shiny and saying, "This Jet, he my best friend!"

We all like Uncle Boon. See those two big teeths he's got in front? He can waggle them, plus his ears too! When we go to Bangkok he carries the whole family around in Jet.

All six! I think he should only take three!? He drives us everywhere, radio blasting pop songs, Jet going "Tuk tuk tuk bang bang!", Uncle yelling and waving to friends and pointing to interesting things for us. Plus all the time Grandma in the back is saying, "Slow down Mister Boon! Slow down!" and poking him sharp with her umberella!

It's all big fun, but really scary!
Now, how about some words for you?

A BIT ABOUT MY TALKING AND WRITING, FOR MY PEN-FRIEND BY SHRIMP

Sometimes it is quite hard for a strange person to learn our speaking because one word can mean a lot of different things. Look, I will show you:

Our word "mai" can mean "wood" or "new" or "burning" or, it can be a question too. It depends how you say it! So if I say to you, "Mai mai mai mai?" it means "New wood burns doesn't it?" but only if I say each mai in a different way! I hope you understand what I mean! Anyway, just in case you would like to have a speak of Thai before you come, here are some easy things:

Yours sincerely, your pen-pien,

Shrimp

24 September

Hello best friend-pen,

Good morning, it's me, Shrimp! How is your weather today? Is it nice and sunny, or is it really chuckling it down like it is here? A big storm is putting rain bombs on my roof right now. It is so noisy I cannot hardly hear my thinks! We're getting lots of rain because it's our monsoon time. It's been pouring for weeks, right back since July!

Yesterday, as I was walking to school with Frog and Finch, there was a thunderstorm that was so enormous it flooded the streets! Before we knew it we were all knee deep in water. Well, actually, I was waist deep. I'm quite small, that's why I'm called Shrimp!

At least the water wasn't cold – our rainy season is nice and warm.

I hear that you begin to get cold weather at this time of year and something called frost. What is it? (Perhaps you could bring me some when you come to Thailand?)

At school today our teacher, Miss Somboon, told us stories about the floods. She said that they are much worse in Bangkok than here and that at one time in 1984 they were so big that water snakes were swimming in the streets and children had to go to school in boats.

Miss Somboon

It's a snake!

Thousands of people went to hospital because the snakes bit them! She also told us how some unlucky people went to flooded telephone boxes and got electricuted when they tried to make phones calls! (Perhaps they were trying to ring the police to tell them about the snakes?)

So now can you see why we build so many of our houses with legs?

Talking about your frost stuff reminders me. In

my other letter I told you about things we have got. Now I will tell you some things that we have not got but you have got, I think. And then you won't be cryings if they aren't here when you come. Tee hee, only a joke!

1) A cold time called winter when pieces of wet, white stuff called snot* falls from your sky. I know about this because I read a story of some English children who built a great big snotman* in their front garden and all the people who passed by said,

It's the most beautiful snotman* we ever did see!

Thanks!

2) At winter I hear you are sometimes walking on your rivers and ponds which have all been turned to frozen hard by coldness in the air, not by the frigerator. It must be very dangerous!

3) Very big noses. I am not being rude but I think our noses look very small next to them. Mine is

only two centimetres big and my mum's is just three. Please measure the noses on your family to make sure I am true?

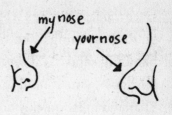
my nose
your nose

4) White hair on some people's heads. Not just for

me with blondey hair!

old people but for quite young and medium also. I think it is called blondey. Have you got any of this sort? We have all got just mainly black.

5) Blue middles to your eyes sometimes. Ours are mostly brown.

6) A time called autumn when all the leaves break from your trees but get put back on again later. How!?

Poo! Stinky food!

7) Strange food called cheese. Frog says it is made from cow milk that has gone bad. Is this true?

8) Cold weather stuff like central heatings, radiators, woolly gloves and hairy underwear.

9) Strange animals called sheeps and rabbits.

I think when my dad and mum were little you had a lot more things that we have not got but since the last 30 years we have been getting all things like Coca Cola, hamburgs and MTV very, very fast! Perhaps you should come to Thailand quite quickly or before we  know it both our countries will be exactly the same. Just another joke! (I think?)

Yours faithfully,

Shrimp

PS Do you like this letter, I did it on mum's PC?

*Mum says you don't build snotmen, you build SNOWmen!

29 September

Dear pen-pal,

Here is the latest news from the Land Of
Smiles. Did you know that is what many
people call Thailand? It is because Thai
people are happy and polite and kind!

   Last night here in Ban Pong it was very, very hot
and sticky, so we left our bedroom windows open
and hundreds of great big beetles flew in and began
whizzing about the electric light bulbs.

   Frog shouted,
"Look, maeng dah!",
then rushed off to
get Dad's big fishing
net and started
catching them.

   "What are you doing that for?" I said.

   "To sell them of course!" he said. "Give me a
hand!" So I did! Lek also joined in the helping but I
think he frightened away more beetles than he
caught! The whole thing was one great hour of mad
crazy fun!

   This morning, on our way to school we took our
maeng dah beetles to the market (we had hundreds of

them). Frog showed them to the lady at the shrimp and noodle stall and told her that she could have them for seven baht each. She said that she would only give four baht for them so Frog and her spent the next few minutes haggling about the price. We do this all the time here when we are buying and selling. I think it is also called bargaining? In the end she agreed to give us five baht each for the man beetles, but not nearly as much for the womens. Guess how she found out which were which? She SNIFFED them!

She sells the maeng dah to people who like eating them. The man ones are supposed to be the tastiest. They're certainly the smelliest! You have to roast them, then grind them up with tomatoes and garlic and chilli and rotten fish. Actually they're delicious!

After we got the money we felt really rich. We bought some fruit juice at the drinks stall but the man

put too much salt in mine (Thai people like a
pinch of salt in their fruit juice). Frog
bought a drawing book, some crayons
for Lek and a new ink pen for me. He
got them all for a really good price!

I hope you will try some roast maeng dah
and salty fruit juice when you come to Ban Pong.

Here is my drawing
of a maeng dah beetle.
What do you think?

By the way it's
raining again. Nice weather for water buffalo!! Which
reminds me, next week we're going to see the water
buffalo racings that always take place at the end of
our rainy season. There isn't room to tell you about
them here so I'll just draw you a picture of a water
buffalo. I hope you like it!

One more bite of news! Our next-door neighbour has just told us that two of their hens were not there this morning, just a few feathers and stuff were on the floor! So we think the big python snake may be still snacking around our village. Uh oh!

Buy for now,

Shrimp

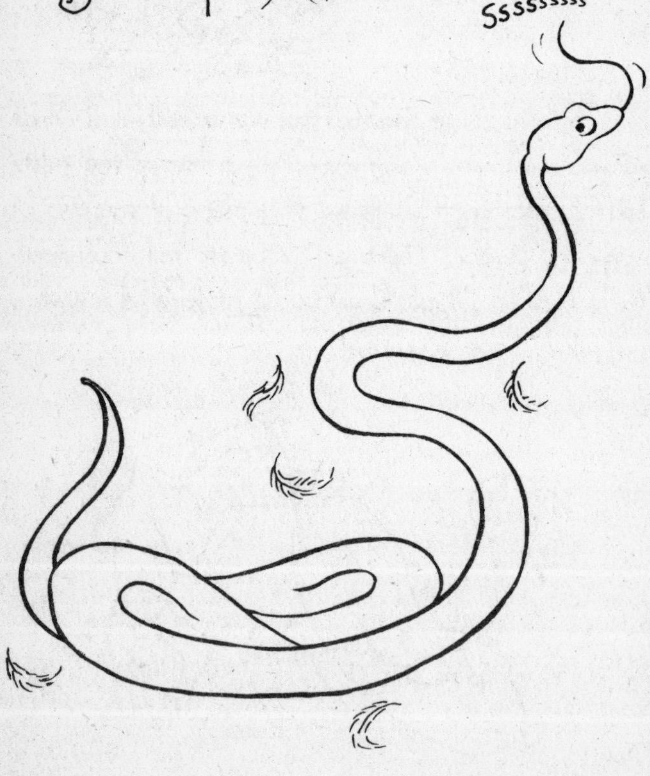

Sssssssss

26 October

Dear pan-fiend,

Sawat dee! (Hello!) In assembly this morning, our Thai flag was run up the flag pole and we all listened to the school band play the National Anthem (do you do this?), then our headteacher read out the list of children who would be cooking the school lunch.

My School

red
blue
white
red
my class
Frog's class

Today it was the turn for me and Finch. We were really pleased because we love cooking. Our teachers buy the ingredients in the market on their way to school then we make the food in the morning.

Today we made stir fried noodles and spicy chicken with coconut and banana pancakes for afterwards (but no maeng dah beetles!). Everyone said it was all completely tasty!

Mmm... I love spicy chicken!

Yummy noodles!

33

Perhaps the next time you cook the lunch at your school you could do these things for your teachers?

Just so you will know what you have got to look forward to eating when you come here Frog has made you a special "All About Thai Food" leaflet. It is with this letter. I have readed it and I think it is great (apart from the dancing fish bit).

All this food talking has given my mouth a real watering, and I can smell delicious perfumes from our kitchen. Mum is cooking fragrant rice, mmm! Now one other thing I got to tell you! Last night the phone rang and Mum answered it. I think it was bad news because she got a worried face very quickly and said "Oh no, that's terrible!" about 15 times! When she had put down the phone she talked quietly to Dad, but not us children. As soon as I find out more I will let you know.

Yours fatfuly,

Shrimp

Mum's fragrant rice - delicious!

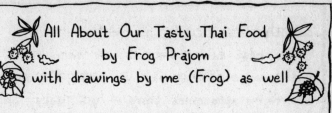

All About Our Tasty Thai Food
by Frog Prajom
with drawings by me (Frog) as well

Thai people love eating. It is sanuk! My dad says there are so many restaurants in Bangkok that you can eat out every night for lots of years without ever visiting the same one two times. We nearly always have rice with our meals – our words for "to eat", "kin khao", actually mean "eat rice".

I love chilli peppers with my food. They are little vegetables that make your mouth feel very hot all over. One of my favourite sorts of chilli peppers is prik kee nuu. This is a rude name, in your language it means mouse poo peppers so you can guess what they look like!

mouse poo peppers

Here is a tip: people from abroad sometimes think their mouth is on fire when they have eaten a hot chilli here so they drink lots of water. Don't do this, it will make it feel worse! Just eat some rice and it will make the hot go away quicker (or just call the fires brigade, hee hee!).

The best eating place I have been to is in the town of Phitsanulok in north Thailand. I ate flying vegetables there – yes really! The restaurant is on one side of the road but the kitchen is on the other. When the vegetables are ready the cook gives a flick of his wok and tosses them all the way across the road to the waiter on the other side! The waiter catches them on a plate then serves them to you! Maybe flying through the air makes them taste better!!

Our food looks nice as well as tasting great. Our fruit and vegetables are carved to look like flower blossoms or pretty leaves. Our mum is good at this. The other day she gave us soup with lovely water lilies floating on it. They weren't real, she'd made them from a cucumber, and she had also decorated the rice with rose buds ... all done from carrots! Does your mum do this?

cucumber water lilies

carrot rose buds →

There are people cooking and selling food everywhere in Thailand. The delicious open air cooking smells coming from the stalls in the streets, train stations and market places will drive you crazy. Just stop and buy a quick scrumptious snack whenever you feel like it.

a tasty snack

No need to worry about plates, your tasty nibbles will come wrapped up in a banana leaf! There are so many tasty and exciting foods in Thailand that your visit can just be a great big eating adventure if you want. Here are just a few interesting and unusual things for you to try:

STICKY RICE

People eat this a lot in Northern Thailand. It is served in a little basket and you eat it with your fingers by rolling it into a ball then

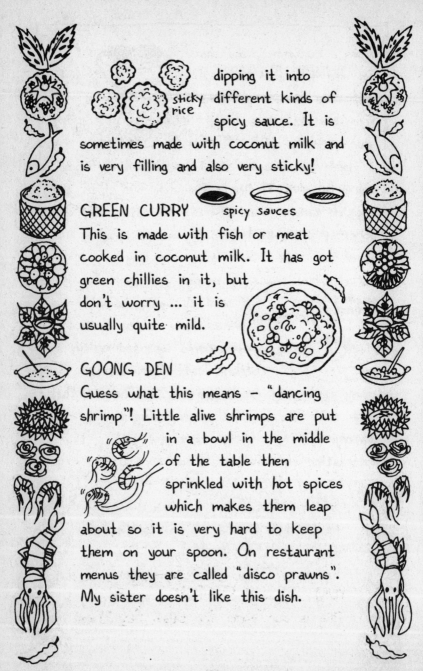

dipping it into different kinds of spicy sauce. It is sometimes made with coconut milk and is very filling and also very sticky!

sticky rice

GREEN CURRY

spicy sauces

This is made with fish or meat cooked in coconut milk. It has got green chillies in it, but don't worry ... it is usually quite mild.

GOONG DEN

Guess what this means – "dancing shrimp"! Little alive shrimps are put in a bowl in the middle of the table then sprinkled with hot spices which makes them leap about so it is very hard to keep them on your spoon. On restaurant menus they are called "disco prawns". My sister doesn't like this dish.

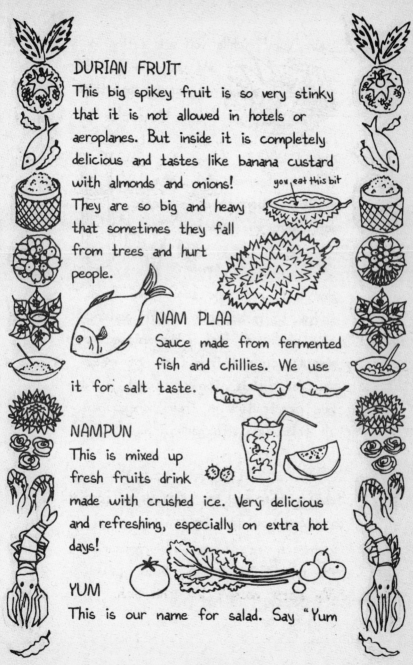

DURIAN FRUIT

This big spikey fruit is so very stinky that it is not allowed in hotels or aeroplanes. But inside it is completely delicious and tastes like banana custard with almonds and onions!

you eat this bit

They are so big and heavy that sometimes they fall from trees and hurt people.

NAM PLAA

Sauce made from fermented fish and chillies. We use it for salt taste.

NAMPUN

This is mixed up fresh fruits drink made with crushed ice. Very delicious and refreshing, especially on extra hot days!

YUM

This is our name for salad. Say "Yum

yum yum!" while you are eating it
and you will probably
get second and third
helps, tee hee!

KHAO LAAM

This is steamed rice served
inside bamboo tubes – please
don't eat the tube!

Bamboo →

And last, here are some Thai food
things to make your mouth water:
raw chickens' feet with onions and
vinegar; curried frog (no, not me!);
stuffed fishes stomach; roast lizard;
bee caterpillars in their honeycombs
all fried up with garlic.

Best wishes, we are all looking forward
to having you for dinner,

Your pal Frog

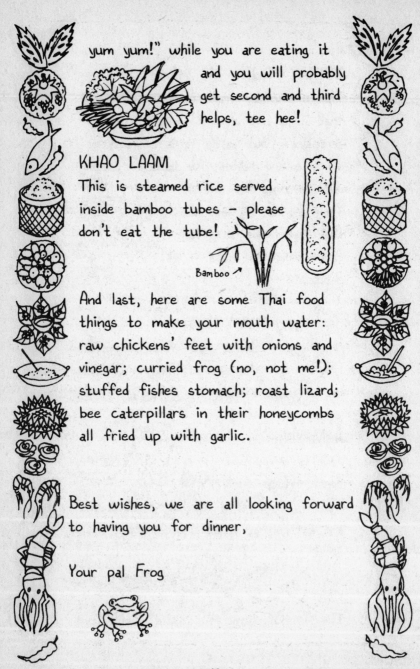

9 November

Dear pen-fiend,

Sanuk mai? How's things in your little spot on the world? Are you having big fun, or is it just fairly ordinary for you? Here in Thailand we are all excited because it is a special time for us. In a few days there will be a full round moon in our sky. It's number 12 we've had this year. When it comes we will celebrate Loy Krathong. This is the time we give thanks for all the rain that has been helping our rice crops grow. Buddhist people believe that the Water Spirits who live in clouds and rivers make all the rain come, so this celebration is to thank them.

It also means the monsoon is almost gone. Hurrah, no more wading! By the way Frog has just told me that the moon we see is the same one that you have. Is this true?

41

At school today we have been making little boats out of banana and lotus leaves. They are called "krathong" and we are going to put a candle, some flowers, three perfume incense sticks and money in them for offering to the Water Spirits. At the festival we will float them on the klong (that's the canal) so watch this space!

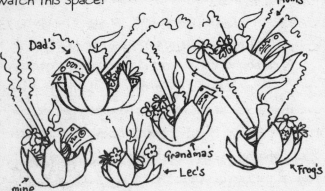

Dad's

Mum's

Grandma's
← Lec's

Frog's

mine

One more thing. Mum has now told me about that phone call. It was a big problem about Uncle Boon, all very sad! I will tell you all about it in my next letter.

Kind regards,

Shrimp

PS No more snake trouble so far, apart from our dog Yip acting a bit nervous!

12 November

Hello again pen-friend,

It's me, Shrimp! Last night, Mum, Dad, Grandma, Frog, Lek and me carried our leaf boats to the klong. Everyone from our town was there too, all chattery and happy! When the shadows went big and the moon came bright we crouched by the water and lit our candles and incenses. Then we sent our krathongs floating off to the dark.

I think the Water Spirits must have been very happy. I know I was! All of a sudden the air was full of perfume smells and hundreds of beautiful leaf boats were bobbling about like twinkly stars. We all cried "Suay-ngam!" (our word for "beautiful!") and "Oooh!" and "Ahh!" (our words for "oooh" and "ahh"!).

It was just like magic! Here is Frog's beautiful picture of it for you.

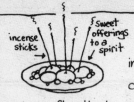

incense sticks →

sweet offerings to a spirit

By the way, do you burn incenses at your special ceremonies?

Now, after the happy news, I will give you the sad Uncle Boon Jet news from that phone call. He has been drowned! No, not Uncle Boon. Jet, his tuk-tuk! Yes, isn't that terrible?

I will tell you how it happened. A few weeks ago in Bangkok there were great big floodings again. Uncle Boon and some other tuk-tuk men were sheltering from the heavy rains at the noodles stall when all of a sudden a huge water wave came racing down the street, no warnings! It was so quick they didn't have time to do nothing but run up some steps to save their lives. The giant flood crashed right into the noodle stalls and the tuk-tuks and next thing, they were all floating away!

After the big water had gone away Uncle Boon ran down the street and found poor Jet in a big wreckage heap, all broken,

downside up and covered with noodles! Our Uncle is now very, very upset because Jet is gone and he cannot do his tuk-tuk work and he had no insurances. Mum has asked him to come and stay with us, so he will be coming next week.

More news soon.

Best greetings,

Shrimp

8 November

Dear pen-friend,

Hello, how are you? What did you have for your breakfast this morning? Our family had delicious spicy rice with plenty of garlics all mixed up with pork and chicken . . . **hot spicy breakfast** and shrimps! As well we had eggs (from our ducks) and cucumbers (from our garden). I helped Mum with the breakfast making.

We used the coriander leaves and lemon grass spices which we grow in pots outside our kitchen door. We made sure that we made an extra big lot of everything so we could give some breakfast to the monks who pass our house each morning.

Do you have monks where you live? We have a lot of them in Thailand and they are very important people here. You will probably see them straight away when you come. They're easy to spot from all the other people because they have bright orange cotton robes and their hair is always very, very small.

When you see them they may be carrying bowls like this:

These are the bowls which Dad and Frog and Lek put the breakfast in this morning. Mum and I aren't allowed to do this because women and girls mustn't touch the monks. Only boys and men can be

a nun →

monks. Girls can be nuns instead if they want. They also shave their heads but wear white robes not yellow ones.

Frog is going to be a monk when he gets bigger. He won't be one for ever though, just for a bit. He has put you some informations about Buddha and monks with this letter for you.

I bet you have by now guessed the other reason we cooked the extra big breakfast? Yes, Uncle Boon is staying here with us. We are being extra good and kind to him too because we want to make him feel better. If we say "Pen yangai (How are you?), Uncle Boon?" he pretends things is all OK, and gives us his big tooth grin, and waves and says "Sabaay dee! (I'm fine!)" but I know really that down deep he is feeling sad inside.

Best wishes,

Shrimp

Now, here's Frog's bit:

ALL ABOUT BUDDHA, AND BEING A MONK BY AROON PRAJOM (FROG)

* In Thailand we have a teacher called Buddha. You will see statues of him all over the place when you come here. Maybe you already know what he looks like? Here's my picture of him in case you don't.
* Buddha lived a long long time ago and was very wise and did a lot of thinking. He thought about how to have a better life, to be a better person and to

make life good for other people — all stuff like that.

* Most Thai people try very hard to do the things that Buddha said were important. I think because of this you will notice that nearly all Thai people are friendly and kind when you come here.

* Thai people believe that you have lots of lives, not just one. They know that if you do good deeds in this life you will have less bad times in your next one. They call doing good deeds making merit.

* Monks study Buddha's ideas and also do quiet thinking for a long time about the problems in the world and good ways to make them better. This is called meditation — even us children do it in school. You should try it some time. Just make your head empty then think quiet calm thoughts. Buddha once did meditating for 48 days without stopping!

Me meditating but NOT for 48 days!

* I will become a monk when I am about 20 years of old. I will be one for three months then I may go to be a soldier in the army for a bit. After this I will probably be a famous cartoon drawer and get married.

* When I become a monk I will have all my hair cut off and live in the Wat. In all of the towns and villages there is a Wat – this is the temple buildings where monks live and do their meditating. You can visit one when you come to Thailand. You will find that it is very calm and peaceful, but before you go in the temple building please remember to take off your shoes.

* When I am a monk I will go out in the morning with my bowl to receive gifts from people who wish to make merit. It's a good thing that people do this: monks have only one meal each day and do not have money and also cannot own anythings but their robes and their bowls. People put many gifts into the bowls — food, incense, flowers, washing powder, Coca Cola, toilet paper, all sorts really!

* Monks aren't allowed to have cars or motorbikes or anything so they have to walk everywhere or just catch the bus (it's lucky they don't have to pay full fares).

* In the old days the monks were teachers to many children in Thailand, but nowadays they don't do this so much but help with building new schools and things instead.

I hope this has helped you learn about Buddha and monks.

Best wishes,

Frog

21 November

Sawat dee dear pen-friend!

It's Shrimp again! Did you know that Thailand is a really big country? Bigger than England and some other places? But not nearly as big as China or America! Miss Somboon says our country is about the same big as France, but different shaped of course. I think we are like an elephant head. Look at the map and see if you think the same!

There are so many exciting things to see in our marvellous country that you will probably be spoilt for choices when you come. So for this letter Frog and me have made this list of really good places for you to visit.

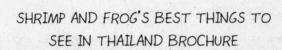

SHRIMP AND FROG'S BEST THINGS TO SEE IN THAILAND BROCHURE

We have been to most of these so we have written down what that we think about them. We didn't always agree on which is best and we also had an argument about if we should put in the Crocodile Farm. Frog won!

Scoring: 1 duck = Quite good, 2 ducks = Very good, 3 ducks = Don't miss!

The Grand Palace, Bangkok –
Frog – This is a special and beautiful real palace with a hundred fantastic glittering buildings all shapes and colours. Our great King is sometimes here: you can visit some parts but

53

please don't go into his bit! It would be quite annoying for him. Please show your respect for this important place and wear smart clothes for your visit.

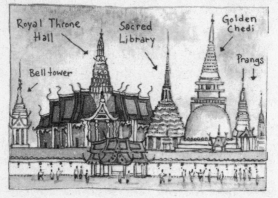

Royal Throne Hall

Sacred Library

Golden Chedi

Bell tower

Prangs

The Wat Phra Kaew Temple –
Shrimp – This temple is next to the Palace (so see them together if you wish!). There are no monks living here but there is a very famous Buddha statue inside. It is the Emerald Buddha which was hidden away but one day lightning struck a very old Chedi (temple) making it crack and there inside was this Buddha which was so wonderful! This Buddha is very small and wears three different robes – one for the rainy season, one for the cool season and one for

the hot season. Our King changes them at special ceremonies.

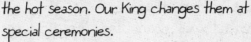

Gilded Altar

Emerald Buddha

Frog's tip – Please remember to take off your shoes before you go in to the temple and make sure you do not point your feet to the Buddha. It's very rude.

The Giant Swing, Bangkok –

Frog – I really like this great big swing in front of Wat Suthat in Bangkok. It was used in a festival in the old days. Teams of young monks took turns to swing on it. They would make it go 25 metres high and try to grab a bag of gold from the top of a bamboo pole – with their teeth!

I would like to have a go but this is not allowed now because of many bad accidents and also the seat has been taken away!

Weee!

Wat Pho – 🦆 🦆

Shrimp – In this temple there is the very biggest Buddha in all Thailand. It's 46 metres long, 15 metres high and Buddha's smile is five metres wide (wider than my classroom!). It is a reclining Buddha (lying down). There are monks living in this temple as well. Do not miss the pond full of turtles!

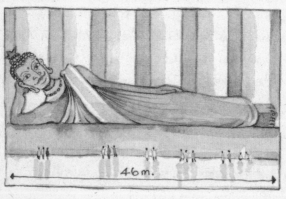

46 m.

The Training College at Surat Thani –

Frog – This is not a college for humans, it is a college for monkeys . . . where they are taught to pick coconuts! They learn for three months and then go to work in the jungle. Some of them can pick one thousand coconuts in one day, but they aren't allowed to keep them! It is real fun and amazing to watch them do their work! I think they must be very brainy!

Shrimp – I felt a bit sorry for the monkeys having to work so hard, but they did seem to be quite happy, I think?

The Floating Market, Damnoen Saduak

Shrimp – This will be very interesting for you because it is just like Bangkok used to be all over when Grandma and Uncle Boon were little. People paddle boats full with heaps of fruits and vegetables and flowers around the klongs. They sell things to each other across the water and to the people who live in stilt houses next to the canals and also to you if you like.

Make sure you go early and be careful not to drop your shoppings!

Frog – I think the floating markets are fun. At one we bought our breakfast from a floating noodle

stall. Our plates of noodles were
passed from one boat to another until
they reached us on the bank!
Also it all makes a nice picture full of
interesting shapes for me to draw and
the boats are loaded with lovely bright
things. Did you like my masterpiece
picture of it!

Ocean World Water Park, Pattaya

Frog –

We visited here on a little
holiday to Pattaya last year. I
think the amazing water
scooters for kids to ride were
the best sanuk thing I've ever
done! It has also got brilliant
giant water slides and, as well,
there is a Bungy jump that
goes the wrong way – up into
the air then back down
again!

Shrimp – 2 ducks. Yes, Nutty and me liked the water park too. I also enjoyed visiting the Mini–Siam model of Thailand. I felt like a giant walking across the whole of my country and got to see 200 of its most famous buildings all in one afternoon! Mum and Dad didn't like Pattaya: too much litter and too many noisy people.

They said they didn't want to come again. Dad enjoyed the golf though and Mum really loved the Orchid Flower Wonderland.

THE CROCODILE FARM, NEAR SAMUT PRAKAN, 30 KM SOUTH FROM BANGKOK

Frog – 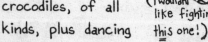 (?)

This is the biggest crocodile farm in the whole world. It has got thousands of crocodiles, of all kinds, plus dancing

(I wouldn't like fighting this one!)

elephants and tame tigers! We saw a man have a wrestling fight with a crocodile! You can buy shoes and bags

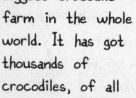

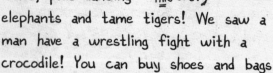

made from crocodile skin there if you like.

Srinthip – NO ducks from me! I didn't like this one bit. I thought it was all cruel and horrible!

The Doll Factory at Bangkok –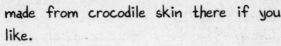

Shrimp – This is my top thing to see in Bangkok. They make beautiful dolls with lovely clothes, all tiny details. Our King gives very special ones to important visitors, and holiday tourists also buy them as souvenirs of Thailand. They are often in our national costumes but also of famous people like Miss Universe beauty queen and the Pope. As well there is a museum with seven hundreds lovely dolls, all styles. So I like to spend a long time looking.

The Snake Farm

Shrimp – This is good. No cruelty to snakes and teaches people all about different reptiles. How to treat snake bites. They make a cure for snake bites here by using poison which they take from snakes.

Frog – for me too! Yes, I agree. We saw them take poison from snakes for medicine and I touched a constrictor (friendly one!).

What a friendly snake!

That's what he thinks!

Hope you have find all this helpful and interesting.

Best wishes,

Shrimp

PS Latest big snake news: three neighbours' hens disappeared and Dad saw some heavy pressed down grass near our pond!

25 November

Dear pen–friend,

How are you? Frog sends his best wishes and Lek wants me to ask you if you have monkeys and crocodiles in your forests and rivers like we do!

Now, I am dying to tell you ~~off~~ of the latest news about a mystery we have got. It is to do with Uncle Boon! This is what has been going on. First of all every morning we have been seeing Uncle Boon going down to the old shed at the end of our garden. Next thing there is a sawing and a big banging all day long.

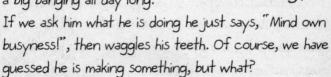

If we ask him what he is doing he just says, "Mind own busyness!", then waggles his teeth. Of course, we have guessed he is making something, but what?

Lek said he thinks he must be building a new tuk-tuk.

"What! A wooden one?" said Frog. "Don't be silly, Lek!"

I said that I thought he might be making a spirit house but Frog said he wouldn't because we have got one, so now we have no idea what he can be up to!

I have just thought of something! You do not know a spirit house, do you? Well, you will be seeing them all over the place when you come here so I better tell you about them quick. They are little houses on poles which look like this. . .

Spirit house

incense

Sweets for the spirits

I do not think that people have them in all countries? Last year a girl called Rebecca from England came in our class at school for a time while her mum and dad were working in Thailand (everyone at our school called her Lebecca because we get your r's and l's sounds mixed up when we try to say them!). Rebecca-Lebecca told me and Finch that she thought that our spirit house was for putting bird food on. When we told her what they were really for she got bad gigglings and went really red.

Spirit houses are very important. We all have them because Thai people believe forests and fields and rivers and things have their own special spirits too, just like people have them!

So, if we dig up a field or chop a tree to make a place to build our own house we will disturb all the spirits that already live in those places. Then the spirits will come and live in our house because we have taken away their home! This can lead to BIG troubles so we must build the phra phum (the spirits) a little house of their own to live in. This is the spirit house. And it is not enough just to make them the house – we must also show them we care about them and put candles and flowers and incense and foods in our spirit house every day.

Frog has done you these pictures to show you how this all happens:

... so we build them a special little house...

Unhappy spirits leave when the trees are cut down...

... which makes them happy again!

By the way, we don't actually see the spirits: they are invisible. But I suppose you knew that anyway!

Best wishes,

Shrimp

PS Last bit of fresh news on Uncle Boon. For a couple of days the making noises have been finished but he is still going to the shed each day, carrying all cardboard boxes and stuff! What is he up to?

28 November

Hello pen-fiend,

Pen yangai (how are you)? Here in Ban Pong
things are very interesting because we have found
out about Uncle Boon's mystery! Two days ago when
I went to feed our ducks, two were missing so Frog
and I had to look for them. We walked around
for ages calling and searching but we
couldn't find them – our
garden is very, very big
with lots of wild
parts. It is also at
the edge of the
jungle.

"I think the big snake has taken them,"
said Frog.
"So do I," I said. "But wait a minute,
what is that noise?" We listened very carefully. Yes,
there was a noise. It was a bird noise, but not really
very ducky or quacky.
"It's coming from the old shed," said Frog.
"Perhaps the ducks are there?"
"Let's take a look!" I said.
Very quietly we sneaked to the shed. The door was

open a bit and the noises were coming from inside.

"Do ducks ever go coo coo coo?" whispered Frog.

"I don't think so," I said. "I've only ever heard

them do quack quack quack."

We creeped up so we could peek in and see what creature could be making the noise. But there was no creature, just Uncle Boon! He was sitting on his seat saying, "Coo coo coo hoo hoo hoo tuk tuk tuk!"

"Why is he doing that?" I whispered to Frog.

"Perhaps all that bad luck tuk-tuk stuff has sent him potty?" said Frog.

"Let's go in and see what his problem is."

But when we walked in the shed straight away we understood everything. On a big shelf opposite Uncle was a beautiful cage with two birds in it. Not ducks but doves! And they were cooing to Uncle Boon who was cooing them back!

"Hello you two!" he said to us. "Meet my new friends. I am teaching them the cooing. I hope your mum and dad won't mind?"

So that is what Uncle Boon has been up to! All those bangings were him making the special big cage and stuff for his new pets. They are not ordinary doves, they are

special Java ones which people
say do bring their owners
good luck! And they are also
special singing doves too!

Uncle Boon is going to put
them in a big dove music competition in February. It
is in Yala in south Thailand. All South East Asia
countries like Malaysia and Burma and Singapore
send their singing doves to there and the prizes are
really big, so we are hoping he does well!

Your pal,

Shrimp

PS We found the ducks. They were on our
neighbour's fish pond. The monster snake hadn't got
them after all!

69

30 November

Dear pen-pal,

Three months have now gone since I started writing
to you. I have known you for ages now. First today
some family news! Mum is busy organizing tourist
people and also planning our big summer holiday for
March. Dad has gone to do some medicine work with
the hill tribe people in northern Thailand. Frog has his
ankle in bandage, he twisted it practising the Thai
kick boxing on a banana tree in our garden, and Lek
has just learned to ride his new bicycle.

Finally, Uncle Boon is happy training his doves to do
musical coos. He has named them Elvis and Tina after
top rock stars from MTV. He is now his old self again
and has been telling us funny stories about being a tuk-
tuk driver in Bangkok. Here is one he gave us yesterday.

One evening he was driving Jet past a big hotel when a farang stopped him (farang is what Thai people call white visitors from over the seas). This tourist man became very rude to Uncle and said, "Hey you old man take me to such and such hotel, I've got an important meeting so be quick about it!" Being quick was not too easy for Uncle Boon because Bangkok was stuck up with huge traffic jams (as usual!) so the man got angry and angrier and was shouting "Go this way! Go that way!" and telling Uncle he was stupid!

When they got to the hotel the man was hopping mad. He jumped out of Jet and said to Uncle, "How much?" and Uncle said, "100 baht (£xxx in your money, I think)." This made the man more angry. He threw the money at Uncle and stamped off but then suddenly stopped and turned to have one last shout at him.

This was a bad thing to do because Uncle had stopped Jet under some trees where big fruit bats have their daytime sleep and it was nearly time for them to get up! Just when the man shouted, Jet also did an extra large bang. All these noises made the bats suddenly fly out of their trees. Not just one or two, but all of them, thousands! And they also did something else! I think you can guess what! So the rude farang was very messy for his important meeting (I hope very smelly too!).

BANG!

split splat!

For Thai people when things get bad we say "Mai pen rai!" which means "Never mind it can't be helped!" and we stay calm cool. Thai people think not getting hot up your collar and having good manners to others is very important, don't you? Sometimes visitors do not know all the ways to do this. Just so you will know I have made this tip sheet to help you.

HOW TO HAVE GOOD MANNERS IN THAILAND
BY S. PRAJOM

Visiting a Thai person's home

Please always remove your shoes before you go in. Try not to stand on the door step because there is a spirit inside it.

With other people

Do not shake hands when you meet someone. Do a wai instead. This is pressing your hands together like this:

Remember always do a wai to grown up before they do one to you!

Feet tips: Thai people do not have a very good opinion of their feets. They think that they are a most lowdown and unimportant part of the body so...

1) Do not point your foot to another person – this is very rude!
2) Do not point your foot to a thing – always use your finger if you have to point.

<u>Head tips:</u> Our head is the most special and top important part of the body and must be left alone! So please do not touch people on the head. Also, if you are with grown ups, try to keep your head lower than theirs (especially old peoples). This is to show your respect and it's not too hard really because grown ups are usually taller than us children.

PAT PAT !

See, it's easy!

<u>At the table</u>
Eat with a spoon and fork except for noodles – these you eat with chopsticks (maybe you need to practise?). Noodle soup you eat with chopsticks and spoon, but you are welcome to try just chopsticks! Hold your fork with your left hand and use it to put the food on your spoon.

Put the spoon to your mouth but do not put your fork in your mouth. Putting a fork in your mouth is bad manners! (Is this the same in your country?)

Eat sticky rice and anything that is with it with just your right hand. Do not clean your plate empty, leave some food

left overs so that it always looks like your very generous, kind host has given you lots too much to eat.

By the way, did you know that about 50 years ago most Thai people ate all food with their bare hands? The old ruler then wanted Thailand to be more like the countries where you are, so he passed a law saying spoon and fork must be used.

Out and about

Twice a day our national anthem is played from loud-speakers at places like the polices and railways stations. When you hear it please stop what you are doing and stand still until it is finished.

I hope all this will all help you and not be too hard to remember for you.

Best luck,

Shrimp

5 December

Hello there pal over the seas,

It's me again, your best pen-pien, Shrimp from Ban Pong!

Today is a great day. It is my birthday. I haven't been to school but instead I have been having lots of sanuk. For my presents I have had some new clothes and a camera.

It has been a very happy day and all over Thailand people have been having a holiday and doing much joyfuls celebrating with fireworks and parades and parties. But not all of it is for me – it is for our King because it is his birthday also! I think I was born lucky to have my birthday on the same day as our great ruler! He is called His Majesty King Bhumibol Adulyadej the Great and this good man is admired and loved and respected by all the Thai people. When you read my story of him I think you will understand why, and be amazed!

ALL ABOUT THE KING OF THAILAND
BY HIS LOYAL SUBJECT, SHRIMP

* Here is his full proper name (I think it might be quite hard for you to say):

Prabaatsomdet
Boramintaramahapumiponadumyadet.

See what I mean!

* When he was younger, King Bhumipol was a monk just like other young men. That's right! He suddenly went from being someone with everything to a person with almost no things. Dressed in his monk's robe he walked in the streets with his alms bowl and was given gifts of food by the ordinary people. Later on, he became King again.

* King Bhumipol cares about all of his people and goes to special trouble to help them. He travels thousands of miles to see the poorest peasants people in his land and talks to them about their problems and gives

them help. He is always thinking up ways to give

everyone a better life. Does your King do these kind things?

* When you come to Thailand you will see King Bhumipol and his beautiful Queen everywhere you go because their picture is put up on the walls in all the shops and hotels, and also everyone has it in their houses too. We are all very proud of them! Do you have pictures of your King and Queen in your houses?

* If you are really lucky when you come to Thailand, you might see the real live HM King Bhumipol going around in his lovely, yellow Royce-Rolls.

Look! It's The King!

There goes our King.

* This is how clever our King is:

1) He can speak in foreign languages as well as Thai.
2) He is a sailor who knows how to drive a big ship.
3) He is a very lovely painter and has his pictures in real artist exhibitions.

* And, as well as all this, he is a really clever musician too! He plays the saxophone and he writes music that is performed in other countries (have you heard it yet?).

* Our great ruler wrote our Royal anthem which is called "Falling Rain". At the beginning of movies the anthem is played and the King's and Queen's picture comes on the screen. We all stand up and keep very quiet for this, so don't forget to do this also if you go to movies when you come here! This wise and clever and kind ruler is a good example to all Thai people. I bet you wish you had a King like ours!

Sometimes visitors from other countries do not know just how important and special our King is to us and do the wrong thing for him. I know this because one windy day in last April, Frog and I saw a tourist woman buying from a market stall. She dropped a 20 baht note on the ground (that's the green one, by

the way). Guess what she did?
She put her foot right on our
King's head! Yes! On the highest
part of the most important
person in Thailand! Frog and I
were very, very shocked, so were
the other people, but the visitor
didn't even notice a thing!

I will stop writing now. I am very tired and not
feeling good in my body this evening. I have got some
pains in my tummy. Maybe I have eaten a bad thing?

Yours fatefully,

Shrimp

4 January

Dear pen-person,

I am writing to you about my sister Shrimp. A few weeks ago she got very very poorly and had to go to the big hospital really fast. She has now had operations to her to make her better. For the moment she is in the intensive caring and has got all sorts of pipes and drips on her and is also completely tired so she will not be able to write to you for quite a long while. She says she

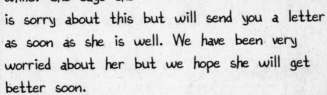

Poor Shrimp

is sorry about this but will send you a letter as soon as she is well. We have been very worried about her but we hope she will get better soon.

Kindest regards,

Frog and all the Prajom family

28 February

Hello pen-pal,

It is ages since I wrote to you. I am sorry! I am lucky that Frog was kind to let you know about me and my ill. Do you remember in my last letter I said I wasn't feeling too good? Well, that was my big sickness beginning. It was called a burst appendix. I had to take it to the hospital and I was there for three weeks. When I came out I had not got it any more! It has taken me all this time to be back to ordinary again. Anyway I am better again and now back to school!

How are you? We have got lots of big sanuk things coming for us now. In just two weeks it will be time for our big summer holidays and also Uncle will be taking Elvis and Tina to the singing competition at Yala. Dad said we will drive them in our big estate car but Uncle has said it is too much trouble for us and him and his birds will fly there instead. They are now all getting in top tip condition for this big challenge! I hope it will be a success!

Now I have to stop this writing because I am not

Plenty of room Uncle Boon!

allowed to get tired. I will do it again soon.

Best wishes,

Shrimp

P.S. When I said that Uncle and the doves are going to fly to Yala I meant in an aeroplane, not by their own wings! I think that the very most south spot of Thailand might be just a bit too far for that sort of flying, especially for my old Uncle! Here is where we are going to for our holiday and also where Uncle is going for his cooing.

1 March

Hello pen-pal,

More problems! It is now just
20 hours before Uncle and
his birds are supposed to be
catching their plane and a
bad thing has happened! Elvis
and Tina are gone! Uncle
thinks that in all the excitement

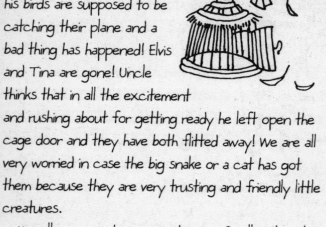

and rushing about for getting ready he left open the
cage door and they have both flitted away! We are all
very worried in case the big snake or a cat has got
them because they are very trusting and friendly little
creatures.

We all are very busy searching so I will not write
more today.

Shrimp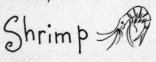

2 March

Phew! Good news! At almost the last very minute we have found Elvis and Tina. Guess where they were? Inside our spirit house eating the fragrant rice offerings I put there for the phum phra spirits! So it is not just Rebecca-Lebecca who thinks they are the birdy houses then, tee hee! Perhaps it is a lucky sign that they were in the spirit house? Anyway, Dad took Uncle, Elvis and Tina to the airport and now they are on their way.

Uncle has been really hoping for big luck this week and he went to see the fortune teller in town who told him good things. So we now hope the best! In just a few days' time our family holiday is going to start. This is the big holiday of the year. School is closed for seven weeks!

We are going to a lovely tropic island in the south part of Thailand called Phuket (you say Poo-Ket). I will send you plenty of writings and do you some photographs on my new camera!

Best wish,

Shrimp

85

15 March

Hello to you from my holiday here at Phuket where it is paradise! Do you like the beautiful beach and jungle trees on my postcard picture? This place is where we have been tonight with Mr Rakthong who looks after the wildlife here and we've had a GREAT adventure. When we got there it was spooky dark and glow flies were glittering in the blackness, just like floating krathong candles!

Mr Rakthong said to us, "Watch that little bit of beach very carefully!"

"All this way, just to look at sand!" whispered Lek, but one moment

later he stopped his fidgets and said, "Wowee! Look at that! The sand is wobbling!"

It was just like mini earthquakes! Something was coming from under the beach! Next moment a small head popped out, then flippers, then a body! It was a baby turtle. A second later another popped up! Then another. And another! Then the beach was wiggling all over with hundreds of baby turtles all scampering to the sea. When they got to the water they started swimming really fast, flippers whirring like they had batteries inside!

It was great to see and I wanted to take a photo but Mum said that I mustn't because the flash-light would be bad for the turtle babies. They find their way to the water by rushing to a bright thing, like the moonlight on the sea, but sometimes when other lights shine (from a hotel or a camera) they scamper to the wrong way then get lost and die.

"How did they all get here?" said Lek.

"Their mum laid her eggs and buried them here a few months ago," said Mr Rakthong. "When these babies have grown they will come back here and lay their eggs in just the same spot. That will not be for another 20 years, so let's hope the beach is still nice and quiet for them and not spoiled by humans!" (People sometimes take the eggs for eating you know!)

We watched the baby turtles for ages and when it was time to go Lek didn't want to and began to cry and stamp his feet. Here is Frog's picture of this great sight (the turtle babies, not Lek stamping!).

Crowds of turtle babies aren't the only amazing animal we've got in Thailand, there are heaps! While we were on our long car trip to here we made you this special Thailand Animals Guide so you will know what to look for when you come. We couldn't get everything in — as well as amazing amphibians, reptiles and mammals we have also got 900 different sorts of birds, more than 27,000 different kinds of flowers and thousands and thousands of insect styles plus stacks of spiders! No wonder people come from all over the world just to see our wonderful nature things.

I'm yawning a bit now, next letter tomorrow (I think).

Best,

Shrimp

PS Here are some glow flies (I think you call them fireflies?) Their back ends shine in the dark!

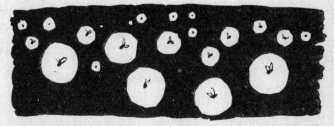

FROG AND SHRIMP'S GUIDE TO
THE AMAZING ANIMALS OF THAILAND

A walking fish

I think these little fish like being on the land better
than being in the water, so they climb out and go
for a walk around! Yes they really do, by using their
fins like little walking sticks. Sometimes they even
climb up trees! If they are frightened they go back
in the water very quickly. We will
probably see some of these on this
holiday. They are sometimes called
mudskippers.

A gecko

These lizards live in houses in Thailand – we've
got some in ours. If you're lucky you will see one
running up the wall or across the ceiling of your
bedroom when you come here. It can't move its

eyelids so it does a funny
thing with its tongue, it licks
its own eyeballs! Uncle Boon
says he can do this too (but
we've never seen him!).

A mouse deer

Believe or not when this deer is full sized it is only 20 centimetres tall to its shoulder! That's not half way up to Frog's knee and even smaller than a small girl called Shrimp! This is the only deer in the world that does not have horns. The babies are kitten size when they are born.

Mouse deer

20 cm

Frog's feet

A giant catfish (plaa beuk)

These are the biggest river fish in the whole world. They weigh 300 kilograms (ten times more than me!) and sometimes they are nearly three metres long (that's three times bigger than Lek!). They are caught in nets – extra big ones! – because many people like to eat them.

It was a plaa beuk... it got away... but it was THIS BIG!!!

OH YEAH!

Slow loris

These are my favourite. They have great big eyes and soft strokey fur, just like a cuddly toy! But

they are not the favourite of the stick insects or the other little animals they like to eat! They move very, very s-l-o-w-l-y.

A hog nosed bat

This is the smallest mammal animal in the whole world. It weighs only two grams and is no bigger than a small butterfly.

Atlas moth

This is one of the biggest moths in the world – the size of a frisbee. Watch out hog nosed bat!

A macaque

There are different sorts of macaque monkeys in Thailand. Some of them

do really crazy things like swimming in the sea and catching crabs to eat.

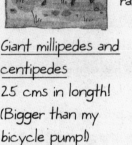

woof
woof!

Barking deer
Yes you guessed, it does bark like a dog! These are rare.

Giant millipedes and centipedes
25 cms in longth!
(Bigger than my bicycle pump!)

Elephants
There are tame and wild elephants in Thailand. The tame ones used to work in the forest moving cut down trees but we don't do this so much now because we are trying to save our enviromoment.

Tigers

There used to be quite a lot of these in Thailand but bad people kill them and sell them. Some people think eating certain bits of tiger is lucky for them.

PS One more big thing before I go to sleep. This morning we had a phone call at the hotel from Uncle Boon in Yala. Great news! Elvis has come third in his competition and Tina has won hers! Uncle is on top of the moon! He has got a big prize money. He is now going back to his house in Bangkok to buy a new tuk-tuk! We will go to stay with him soon. Hurrah!

Such clever doves!

16 March

Hello pen-friend,

Today I thought I would send you this map of
Phuket. Do you like the little pictures?

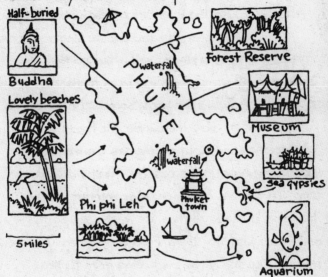

We have been to a different beach and done
sports and swimming and seen a man fall off his jet
ski (he wasn't hurt). On this beach there were lots of
holiday makers from Australia and Germany and
England (you may probably know some of them). Many
of them were rubbing white juice on their bodies then
laying very still in the sun for a long time, like big
pink lizards. We thought this was very funny!

"Why are they doing that?" whispered Frog.

"Because they want to change colour," said Mum. "It is called sun-bathing."

"You're joking!" said Frog.

Most Thai people don't do this sun-bathing thing. Do you?

After watching the interesting beach people for a bit we went to the Wildlife Visitor Centre and watched a film of the interesting mum turtles laying their eggs, so now I can tell you how the babies got there!

When they come out of the sea the mums first have to struggle up the beach to find a dry bit of sand. Turtles are made for swimming not walking (they spend nearly all their life in the sea) so this is a really hard work for them. Frog and Lek and me know this because today we tried being mum turtles flopping our way up the beach. It was very hard work! Like this. . .

96

When the mum had finished digging a hole
with her back flippers she started to lay her eggs.
It seemed to go on for ever!

". . . eighty-six, eighty-seven, eighty-eight!" counted
Frog. "How many more?"

"Sometimes they lay more than one hundred," said
Mum.

"What a lot of children's names to remember!" laughed
Dad. "And all with the same birthday!"

"Will she ever see her babies?" I said.

"I don't think so," said Mum.

"Oh look! She's crying!" said Frog.

He was right. The mum turtle had finished covering her
nest with sand and was flopping back to the sea with big
tears rolling down her face.

"She's probably sad that she will never see her children
grow up," I said (feeling a tear come to my eye).

"Don't worry, it's not that," said Dad. "The tears
are to wash away the sand that she got in her mouth
and eyes while she was digging her nest."

New letter tomorrow. Hope you are all well,

Shrimp

I will send you some sunshine, tee hee!

97

22 March

Dear penny-friend,

I don't want this holiday to finish, we are having too much fun!

Phi phi Leh

Today's adventure was to the beautiful island you can see in this picture which is called Phi Phi Leh (you say Pee Pee Lay). That longtail boat is taking our family and some other people to a spooky cave there. Can you see Frog and Lek and me fun dangling over the side? We were spotting all the amazing fish that were swimming right next to us. The water here is so clear that you can see to the bottom, no problem! Here are some of the fishes we saw:

angel fish

parrot fish

golden butterfly

clown fish

My favourite fish were clown fish and I had to take some photographs of them. When a big lot of them swam past I pointed my camera and clicked but then my lovely new camera fell from out of my hands and was tumbling through the water with the clown fish!

"They probably think it's a camera fish!" laughed Frog, but I didn't laugh because I was crying! The boat man's helper saw I was upset. He said, "Mai pen rai!" then dived into the water. A moment later he was back with my camera!

I think it will be all right, Mum says it's waterproof. I hope so! I was really glad to get it back because just then everyone got excited and cried, "Look, look!" and some silver birds jumped out of the sea and flew beside our boat! But they weren't birds, they were flying fish! They whizzed through the air with their fins stretched, then splashed back into the water. I think they were showing off!

I don't know how my photos will look because it was quite hard to keep my camera pointed on them. I'll send you some when they're ready and you can tell me what you think! Have you ever seen a real flying fish?

Mum has just told me I must stop writing now because we are going to a restaurant to have giant crabs cooked on beach fires. Tomorrow I will tell you about the strange goings-on in the cave.

Best friend,

Shrimp

23 March

Dear pal,

Hello, I'm here again. Now I will finish telling you my cave story. Me and Frog are sitting under this big beach umbrella all nice and warm and comfortable – which it really wasn't in that big dark cave I am telling you about! It felt very, very cold and nasty when we went into it after our sunny boat ride, plus there were lots of spooky squeakings and twitterings from the birds who live there, and squirmings and jigglings under our feet from the cockroach beetles on the floor! It all gave me the shivers. When we got our eyes used to the dark this is what we saw:

Bamboo pole ladders tied with creepers

very rickety ladders

Tap tap tap

Squeak!

Chao Ley

Squeak!

Hello!

"What's that man doing?" whispered Lek.

"He's going to pick the birds' nests so he can sell them to people who like to eat them in soup," said Mum.

"Eat nests?" said Lek.

"Yes, they are supposed to give you energy and special powers," said Dad.

"Well, when I get home I want to collect nests and eat them too!" said Lek.

"You can only eat these ones," said Mum. "They're made from bird spit. The cave swifts weave it to a cup shape and it goes hard in the air."

Bird's nest made from tasty bird spit!

"It's not fair to the swifts!" I said.

"It's all right, they build another nest," said Dad.

"But don't they take that too?" I said.

"Well, yes," said Mum. "But then they build another one and the Chao Ley leave nest number three alone!"

"Three times lucky for people, three times lucky birds!" said Frog.

You will probably now be wondering what are the Chao Ley so I will tell you about these very amazing humans. Their name means water people and sometimes they are called sea gypsies because many of them don't stay in one place all the time.

The Chao Ley are wandering people who go all over the place but always live in their boat-houses. The sea gypsies have got their own special language. They look quite a bit different to other Thai people too. Their hair has a red colour instead of black. Their skin is also much darker than other people's. I think this is probably because they are out in the sun much more.

I know they are very clever and brave. As well as doing daring-devil climbing up the caves and the cliffs they also do daring-devil diving to look for pearls and shells on the seabed, but without aqua lungs and stuff! They dive down really deep then walk along the bed of the sea, just like me or you going for a nice stroll along the beach! Here is Frog's picture of them doing a fish hunt.

It looks like an old-fashioned Thailand tiger hunt, but all happening many metres under water!

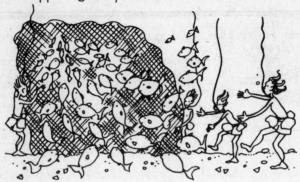

Mum told me about some Chao Ley people who live on Phuket and now just stay in one place. There are

always big buses parked near their homes with tourists noseying at them and giving them sweets and money to be in photographs, like they are stupid children! I really don't think this is too nice at all. Just imagine having people always coming to your house and school and staring at you every day!

Now, one more amazing thing we saw from our boat yesterday is a whole village built on sticks in the sea. Everywhere was on poles – the school, the shops and even the sports field. Some children were playing football on it and when one scored a goal the keeper had to jump in to the sea to get the ball. It all looked like great fun to me!

Village in the sea.

Football pitch

ball

What a pity this holiday has come to its end!

Best wishes,

Shrimp

27 March

Dear pencil-friend,

High there! We're all back home in Ban Pong now. Have you started doing your kite flying yet? Here the winds have come so we've all gone kite crazy!

From my window I can see flocks of waW (our word for kite) dancing across our bright blue sky. They're all shapes and sizes: birds, snakes, fishes, funny faces, every kind! Some are real giants, ten metres big (higher than my house, no kidding!) and some are just centimetres. Mine is a green and red butterfly one. I'm going to fly it after this letter is done.

It's not just us children who are kite crazy in Thailand, it's grown-ups too. My dad and his friends are getting ready their special big man kite now. It's called a "chula". It is a giant star shape.

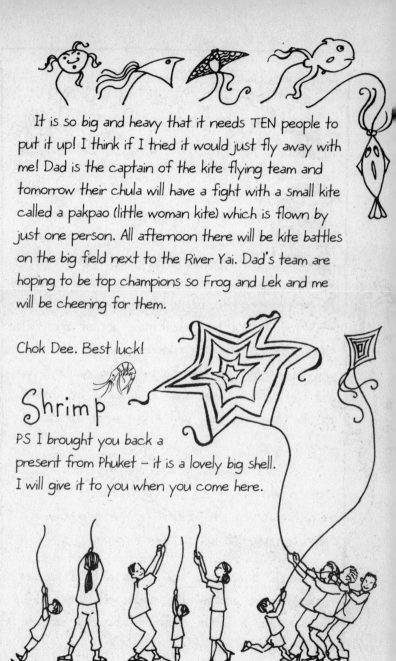

It is so big and heavy that it needs TEN people to put it up! I think if I tried it would just fly away with me! Dad is the captain of the kite flying team and tomorrow their chula will have a fight with a small kite called a pakpao (little woman kite) which is flown by just one person. All afternoon there will be kite battles on the big field next to the River Yai. Dad's team are hoping to be top champions so Frog and Lek and me will be cheering for them.

Chok Dee. Best luck!

Shrimp

P.S I brought you back a present from Phuket — it is a lovely big shell. I will give it to you when you come here.

28 March

ON THE SPOT SPORTS NEWS
by Miss Shrimp & Mister Frog,
Top Radio Ban Pong reporters

Miss Shrimp: Well here we are today at
the big field. Lots of happy people are
getting down their picnics and watching
the kite fun: fighting for kites, plus judging
for best looking kite. Yes, a kite beauty contest!
Mr Frog: A line has been made across the field.
First kite to pull its opponent across the line
will be winner of the fighting. The chula is up
and the captain (our dad) is blowing his whistle
to his team so they will know what to do.

pakpao   chula

The little pakpao is up — its skilful handler
is dodging it around the chula. It looks
cheeky like a little mosquito buzzing around
a big angry elephant!

Miss Shrimp: The chula tries to catch the little pakpao with the bamboo hooks on its line but the nifty-swifty pakpao has nipped out of his clutches again! And now, what's this?

Mr Frog: Oh no! The pakpao has hooked the chula. The chula captain is blowing his whistle and jumping about like crazy. His team are struggling hard but it is no good, she is pulling him across the line. And now . . . CRASH! The chula is down! Big roar from pakpao supporters and big groans from chula fans (us!). Oh well, mai pen rai! Stop crying, Shrimp!

Did you like the report? It was a bit of sanuk fun, but a pity for Dad.

Old days —

War kites carried big jars full up with gun powder – flying towards enemy – fuses fizzling

then ...

K E R P O W !!!

... bombed them!

Old days — for telling when monsoon winds will come.

Old days – to frighten away evil spirits by making noises.

"tink tink

"tink tink

rustle

Ceremony Kites – Jingly bells and lamps attached – look lovely and sound nice.

Bird-scaring kites – farmers fly them over rice paddies.

And now perhaps you are scratching to go out and fly your own kite? I hope you have got the wind.

Best wishes,

Shrimp

12 April

Hello friend,

Phew! Very hot today! The scorching weather is now here. Even Thai people are saying it's too hot! My thermometer was to 36°C this morning. What does yours have on it? Now I am having three showers each day to keep myself fresh. Well, tomorrow is our Songkran festival so we can have a cool relief. It is our celebration to welcome the Thai Buddhist New Year which begins in this month. It means "Changeover", like a big clean start when we all get ready for new rains, new rice, new everything really! And also get very, very WET! This is what happens . . .

SONGKRAN
by S. and A. Prajom

First day. Give our houses a tops to bottoms clean. Get new clothes. Fresh start for all!
Second day. We are as busy as beasts in the kitchen getting food ready to give to

111

the monks. We also get presents ready for old folks and important people (to show our respect). We build little temples from sand then decorate them with star pictures and coloured paper flags. They are all in little rows and look lovely!

Third day. It is time to make merit. We take food and robes to the temple and give them to monks. People also buy little animals, like birds in bamboo cages, little fish and turtles in poly bags, from stalls outside the temple. Then they set them free in the klong (not birds though!) so they will have a better life. Frog says he thinks the people who sell them nip out and catch them again so they can sell them lots more times to make extra moneys? If they do, I don't think this will do them much good in their next life, do you?

<u>Fourth day</u>. To pay our respects to old people we do things like bathing their hands in scented water, to show them we care and know they are very wise and clever. We also wash our Buddha statues with perfumed water. There is a procession with music, and a beauty contest too! I love this – am planning to be in it (and the winner!) when I am a bit older! Also there is lots of getting wet! As well as being New Year, Songkran is the water festival.

We are expecting the rains soon so I think perhaps all the water goings-on is to help the rains. No rains means our rice won't grow and then all Thailand will be in big trouble! Our Songkran water fun starts off slowly, just polite stuff like having nice-smelling water tipped on you from silver bowls (please don't forget, you are supposed to stand still for this!), but, by the last day everyone goes water-throwing crazy. They use everything they can get their hands on – jugs, water pistols, buckets, pumps, hose

pipes, the lot! I will tell you all about this in my next letter.

Good wishes,

Shrimp

14 April

Hello again!

First thing this morning Frog and
Lek and me were standing by our
bedroom window with a big bucket
of water on the ledge. When Mr
Sudham walked beneath us we
tipped the whole lot on to him and
shouted "Sawat dee Pee mai!"
(That's "Happy New Year!")
You should have seen him. He
jumped two metres in the air
and when he came down he looked all wet and funny!
When he saw who had done it he shook his fist to us
and pulled an angry face, but then he said "Sawat
dee Pee mai!" and laughed. Oh, I forgot to tell you,
Mr Sudham is our headmaster!

By the way, this letter nearly got a soaking as well!
All today it has been one long water battlement

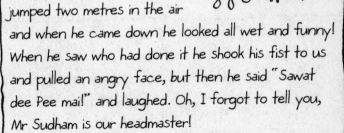

going on everywhere! When Mum drove
into work she even got a face full
from her workers (she'd forgotten
to close her car window). In our
village everyone was slinging water on

everyone else and we didn't mind one little bit. It's so nice and cooling! Just to make sure no one runs out of ammunitions there are water barrels put all around town for refills. So everyone can go water fight mad!

One sad thing! Frog drew a great picture of the water fights for you, but guess what? Yes, that has got soaked too! So he has done you another one. It still looks quite good.

Does your headmaster get angry if you throw water all over him? Have you got a festival like Songkran? If you haven't you should have. It is a lot of fun! Having fun is very, very important and we all work very hard to make it happen! My dad says, "What is life without 'sanuk'?"

My next letter to you will be from Uncle Boon's in Bangkok — we are going to stay with him!

Best wishes,

Shrimp

PS Sawat dee Pee mai!

Uncle Boon's new tuk-tuk

5 May

Hello there,

First of all here is some news which is good and bad.
At school we will soon start rehearsals for a big play
and I am very pleased to tell you that Miss Somboon
has chosen me for one of the top acting and dancing
parts in it! Also my mum has been really excited by
my letters to you and now she has asked me and Frog
to help her make a special "Thailand For Children"
brochure for her tourist work. I am very happy and
proud about both of these things but I am also sad to
tell you that they are going to take away all of my
time for writing to you. So I am ~~frightened~~ afraid
that this will be almost my last letter to you. But not
quite — so I must makes the most of it!

Now, do you know the picture? Yes it's Bangkok, our capital city! We are having a great time here on our visit to Uncle's. He has been driving us around in his brand new tuk-tuk – and guess what it is called – yes, Jet Two!

Today we all went to a ceremony where a man planted special rice to make all Thailand have a good rice crop this year. At the end everyone ran on to the field and picked some up.

It's very lucky, you know! I got eight grains but Frog couldn't find any so I gave him one of mine. I am going to plant mine in our garden. One for each person of my family and one for you, of course! I am sure they will bring us all good fortunes!

It was very hot at the ceremony but this evening we have had a big storm which made it a bit cooler. It was the first of this year's monsoon rains! That is amazing! It seems only five minutes since I was telling you about them last year! Have I really been writing to you for that long?

Bangkok is huge, bigger and noisier than anywhere

else in Thailand, and it's got a very big name! Not Krung Thep, which means City of Angels. That's just its short name. The full name is 41 words, the longest place name in the world! I think it's also got the longest traffic jams as well – Dad says they are. Uncle Boon says Bangkok hasn't always been full of smokey traffic. He remembers how it used to be and has asked us to send you his special memories of the old days (which he's written with a lot of help from me and Frog).

My childhood memories of old days Krung Thep by Uncle Boon

Hello there farang child, howdy do! When I was little boy Krung Thep was all water, hardly any roads, just klongs. All our houses was standing on big sticks in water. All very good and useful: we had water for travelling, swimming, cooking, washing dishes, clothes, pans and selves! All kids ran straight out front door then, SPLOOSH

120

SPLOOSH SPLOOSH straight aways we are having water fun in klong, and getting clean!

For going to places we always went on our little boats. Also there were many boat people passing our doors selling noodles, bananas, pineapples, rice, silk, everything. No getting stuck in stinky traffic jams to go to market like nowadays, just great big boat jams!

When I was born guess what they did with me? They chucked me in canal! This protects me from bad diseases. I think many Thai people are amphibians, half human half fish! One day the big frog* said, "Get rid of klong! Build road instead!" so now we're number two traffic jam place in the whole world! I think it still wants to be a klong place, that's why it does floods at monsoon to tell us so. Also did you know whole city is sinking - five centimetres a year!

Best wishes,

Uncle

Do you like my new tuk-tuk?

   I hope you enjoyed Uncle Boon's memories. He's funny, isn't he?

Your pal,

Shrimp

PS * Big frogs is what Thai people call the top bosses who have great power.

18 May

Hello pen-fiend,

 I am down in the dumplings because this is my last letter for you. I can hardly believe it! Well, here goes.

We are back home from Uncle Boon's and the storm clouds are getting bigger and bigger, and more rains each day. It is the time of planting and growing for us so we have put the lucky grains in the soil. I have not forgotten your special one. What things are you planting in your garden now, anything good to eat?

When we got back from Uncle's there was a parcel with a postcard waiting for us. It was from our cousin Daeng, who lives in Yasothon Province in the North-East, I-saan part of Thailand (just about where the ear is on our elephant head shape).

123

Yasothon is very hot and dry and a very tough place to live. I would not like to be cousin Daeng one bit! Sometimes the rains do not come when they are supposed to and the rice does not grow so Daeng and his family have nothing to eat but frogs and lizards and ants with some chillies!

Now I will tell you about what was in the parcel. It was a birthday present from Daeng's mum. It is a beautiful scarf and it is made from silk. Daeng's mum and all the other women in their village have the job of weaving things out of silk threads which are made for them by thousands of caterpillars! To help you understand this very amazing thing Frog and I have made this picture story for you – our last thing of all!

SILK WORMS

1) The mum silk moth lays her eggs on the leaves of mulberry bushes. They are so small you can hardly see them.

2) Tiny caterpillars come out of the eggs and eat the leaves. "Munch munch." These caterpillars are called silkworms.

3) After only about three weeks of munching the silkworms have grown to about six centimetres long! But they still carry on eating. "Munch munch munch."

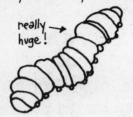
getting bigger

4) After more eating "Munch munch munch munch!" the silkworm is fully grown. It is now ten thousand times bigger than when it was born!

really huge!

(Frog and I are glad we are not ten thousand times bigger than when we were born!)

5) It is now time for the silkworm to build itself the little house called a cocoon. It makes whitey yellow thread come from its mouth really fast (12 centimetres comes out every a minute!) then wraps it around itself.

6) Now that it is inside its cosy little packet the silkworm begins to change into a moth. This takes between two and seven days but. . .

wrapped up and cosy

7) Now comes the horrible sad part! Before the caterpillar has time to change into a moth the cocoon

cocoons on a tray

boiling water

special fork
large thread
single threads
cocoons

is put into hot water and it dies.

8) Daeng's mum or one of her friends now unwraps the silk cocoon thread. There is loads of it – the caterpillar has wrapped itself in nearly a whole kilometre of silk!

9) Two or three silk threads are twisted together to make one very strong thread.

10) Silk is very tough and also very comfortable.

Here I am in my traditional Thai silk costume.

Many people say that silk from Thailand is the best in the world. Do you or your family have any Thai silk clothes? If you have perhaps they are made from silk from Daeng's mum's caterpillars.

PS Did you know that the bark from old trees where the silkworms live is crushed to make the paper for Thai umbrellas?

So that is it, the end of my letters to you. Well, for some time being anyway. I am now very very sad, but also very very happy because I am so glad that I decided for you to be my best pen ~~chump~~ chum in the first place. I have had so much sanuk telling you about my life and my country and I hope you have enjoyed it all as much as I have. Maybe one day we will meet when you come to Thailand, or perhaps when I come to your country.

Frog sends his best wishes and so do all my family and Finch too. And by the ways, if you do bumps into Rebecca-Lebecca, please give her my best greetings and tell her about the Elvis and Tina spirit house, it will give her the giggles.

Thaibye!

I will keep looking at your rice plant for you and think of you whenever I go to our garden to check it out. Which reminds me, we never did see that big snake again, thank godness! Anyway I really must go now, I can hear mum calling me to feed the ducks. And guess what, it has just started raining again!

Thaibye,

Shrimp

SSss SS S sssssss

127

AIRMAIL FROM...

Would you like to read airmail letters from children in other parts of the world?

Airmail From Africa - *Ngorongoro - where cow poo is lucky!* Meet Christopher from Tanzania. He's dying to tell you all about his life in Africa, his family, his village, his school and his very special cows.

Airmail From South America - *Amazonia - where tree frogs go moo!* Maria and Leo are twins from Copacabana in Brazil. They are going on a brilliant adventure trip to the Amazon Jungle, and they're writing to tell *you* all about it.